André Breton

by J. H. MATTHEWS

Columbia University Press

NEW YORK *&* LONDON 1967

COLUMBIA ESSAYS ON MODERN WRITERS is a series of critical studies of English, Continental, and other writers whose works are of contemporary artistic and intellectual significance.

Editor: William York Tindall

Advisory Editors

Jacques Barzun   W. T. H. Jackson   Joseph A. Mazzeo   Justin O'Brien

André Breton is Number 26 of the series.

J. H. MATTHEWS, Professor of Romance Languages at Syracuse University, is the author of *An Introduction to Surrealism, An Anthology of French Surrealist Poetry,* and *Surrealism and the Novel.*

Copyright © 1967 Columbia University Press
Library of Congress Catalog Card Number: 67–16892
Printed in the United States of America

André Breton

Born at Tinchebray (Orne) in 1896, André Breton embarked upon premedical studies at the age of seventeen, only to discover that medicine was to be, for him, but "an alibi." His true vocation was poetry.

Breton's first models were a curious medley of poets. Clearly, he did not yet know what kind of poems he wished to write. It is true of course that, considered in retrospect, his admiration for certain aspects of the work of J. K. Huysmans and for Gustave Moreau takes on anticipatory significance: "The discovery of the Gustave Moreau museum, when I was sixteen," Breton wrote in 1961, "conditioned for always my way of loving." We cannot but notice, though, that the young Breton respected at the same time Mallarmé, Viélé-Griffin, and Jean Royère. Among his first publications was a sonnet printed in *La Phalange*, beneath a dedication to Paul Valéry. Yet, although Breton hardly knew the work of Rimbaud, one may detect in him a restlessness regarding the nature of poetry which very soon was to make him attach particular meaning to Rimbaud's gesture of turning his back upon literature, as well as to Valéry's prolonged silence from the year 1892.

Called to service in the 1914 war, Breton found himself precipitated into a mode of existence from which he received a psychological jolt severe enough to make him readily responsive to two new attractions, which were to take him from the path of symbolism: Guillaume Apollinaire and Jacques Vaché. Prophet of modernity, acutely sensitive to new developments in art and literature, Apollinaire helped to show Breton where he might satisfy his thirst for something new. Meanwhile Vaché, whom Breton met in Nantes in 1916, exercised no less significant an influence upon him. In Vaché, iconoclasm, displayed in a destructive form of humor he called "umour," combined with a contempt for literature which fascinated Breton. "But for him," the latter was to remark later, "I would have been a poet." Mistrustful by now of the conventions of established literary forms that seemed to debase the title of poet to the point at which he felt compelled to reject it, Breton found himself better prepared, as the war progressed, to accept a new influence, that of total revolt against all literary and artistic pretension, stridently expressed in the first two numbers of a review called *Dada*, which he read in Apollinaire's apartment.

Breton was acquainted already with Philippe Soupault and Louis Aragon. Together they had founded a magazine ironically entitled *Littérature*. Appearing for the first time in March, 1919, *Littérature* serialized in its first four issues the *Poésies* of Lautréamont, copied by Breton from the only known copy, in the French National Library. Yet while the inclusion in *Littérature* of Lautréamont's text is a fact of signal importance for those concerned to trace the trend which Breton's evolution as a writer was beginning to take, the presence in the magazine of material signed by Gide, Valéry, Giraudoux, and Drieu La Rochelle is proof enough that regard for tradition still counted for Breton and his friends. An example of integral revolt was needed still, to release them from remaining traces of respect for convention. Such an example was supplied by a group of writers and artists in Zurich, whose activities were mirrored in the review *Dada*. When Tristan Tzara, a leading dadaist and author of a celebrated Dada Manifesto dating from 1918, arrived in Paris, he was greeted, Breton has recalled, "like a Messiah."

It appears beyond question that Breton's participation in

[4]

dadaist activities in Paris, from 1919, helped to liberate him from residual influences which would have impeded the full development of his poetic independence. For a while, in fact, Breton's fidelity to dadaism could not be challenged. Gradually, however, he reached the conclusion that dadaist practice limited its ambition to a destructive program, precluding the possibility of advance beyond negation. What is more, he was alarmed as early as August, 1920, by the sympathetic tone Jacques Rivière adopted, when discussing dadaism in *La Nouvelle Revue française*. Dada, it appeared, was not only ceasing to progress beyond limited success; it was in imminent danger of becoming respectable, and of being assimilated with literature.

After his withdrawal from dadaism in 1922, Breton deemed it profitable to attach increased importance to various experiments in writing in which he had participated even while playing a role in dada's resistance to convention. There is evidence of this experimentation in *Littérature*, despite its having become the organ of dadaism in Paris. Reflection upon the material in question—the most impressive single text was *Les Champs magnétiques*, published by Breton and Soupault in *Littérature* at the end of 1919—induced an effort on Breton's part to consider the nature of the results obtainable by methods so far used only haphazardly. This effort culminated in October, 1924, in the *Manifesto of Surrealism*, which rallied around Breton several ex-dadaists and some new allies.

Consideration of the full consequences of the assertion of liberty which Breton made in the name of surrealism is impractical in the present context. It is sufficient to say of the first *Manifesto of Surrealism*, as of the *Second Manifesto* (1930), that its author neither condescends to engage in discussion, nor aims at persuasion. From the moment when surrealism became articulate, jibes about the weakness of its program and about the instability of its foundation in reason or philosophical argument have left its defenders unperturbed. Typical of their attitude is the complete disregard for adverse criticism evidenced in Breton's manifestoes. In these texts, with a logic for which he has been given too little credit, he makes an impassioned appeal to those impulses in man which come from a predisposition to cast off the restrictions of the rational universe. Breton consistently addressed himself only to those eager to accept surrealism's invitation to explore in directions in which reason places no trust. The sources of the vitality of the surrealist spirit lie here, as does the origin of the attraction exercised for four decades by the example of Breton's published works and magnetic personality.

Nevertheless, the rank of leader of the surrealist group was not an entirely enviable one. Natural as it may seem to critics to select Breton as an exemplary surrealist figure, repeated reference to his work as simply a convenient source of information on surrealist attitudes has the unfortunate effect of reducing his status to that of theoretician. The result has been relative neglect of the creative elements in his writing. All too frequently, critics ignore the fact that Breton practiced surrealism as ably as he preached it, and that no assessment of his contribution to surrealism will be complete until his achievements as a poet have been established.

A narrower focus than is usually employed, while it may seem to limit the significance of what Breton had to say, commends itself, to the extent that it allows us to resist, so far as possible, the temptation to read *through* the prose works of Breton, rather than to relate them to the state of mind in which his poetry was produced. These essays can then be seen to cast light upon the poetic sensibility of their author, and to make

[6]

possible a better understanding as much of the nature of his poetic effort as of the impulses and aspirations which gave it life. As Breton himself wrote in his preface to Max Ernst's *La Femme 100 Têtes:* "The particular truth of each of us is a game of patience in which he must, from all others, and without ever having seen them, seize the elements in flight." It is to *Nadja*, to *Les Vases communicants*, to *L'Amour fou* and *Arcane 17* that we must first look for the rules of the game of patience which Breton, as poet, played for over forty years.

In 1926 Breton's *Légitime Défense* declared, in the name of the surrealists, "It seems to us that revolt alone is creative." The following year the antirational stress of the *Manifesto* was confirmed by his *Introduction au Discours sur le Peu de Réalité*. Meanwhile, Breton was facing the problem of applying surrealist principles to the practice and evaluation of painting, in a series of articles written for the magazine *La Révolution surréaliste*, which replaced *Littérature* in 1924. These articles were published separately, under the title *Le Surréalisme et la Peinture*, in February, 1928.

Well before 1928, in other words, surrealism had become for Breton the only possible answer to the problem of man's relationship to a world where everything conspires to frustrate his desires. If we consider the implications of the direction Breton's thought was taking in the mid-twenties, it is fair to conclude that he was in some danger of finding his situation difficult. Rejecting as valueless the purely realistic depiction of the world, Breton nonetheless required the satisfaction of needs which, if definitively alienated from reality, must end in frustration. At the same time, of course, in continued aversion to literature, Breton esteemed the act of writing, and even more that of publishing, to be pure vanity. In the circumstances, it is

[7]

permissible to ask, firstly, why he wrote *Nadja* and, secondly, why he published it in May, 1928.

In *Nadja* Breton gives attention to a succession of unexpected incidents, curious coincidences, and inexplicable occurrences he has witnessed—events that "do not permit our return to reasoned activity except, in most cases, if we appeal to the instinct of self-preservation." In the perspective of the preoccupations thus betrayed in the early pages of his book, it must have seemed to Breton a notable sign of the beneficent intervention of chance in human affairs when, in 1926, he met a young woman calling herself Nadja, "because in Russian that's the beginning of the word hope, and only the beginning."

The fascination of the unrelated events assembled in the early pages of *Nadja* is brought into focus when Breton gives attention to the mystery of Nadja, "free from all earthly bonds, so little does she belong, but marvelously, to life." Anticipating one of the major themes of *Arcane 17* (1944), Breton borrows from Celtic mythology the figure of Melusina, to render the strange attraction of Nadja. As the incarnation of Melusina, Nadja represents the union of opposites, and hence the reconciliation of the world of desire with that of reality. She is for Breton a figure of interrogation. He does not omit to note, therefore, that when she arrived in Paris for the first time, the illuminated sign of the Sphinx Hotel, on the Boulevard Magenta, induced her to take a room there. Meeting her the day after presenting her with a copy of *Les Pas perdus* (1924), he notices that she has the book open to a text recounting a meeting which, within a few moments of one another, he, Aragon, and André Derain each had with an unknown woman. The significance of the enigmatic question that the sight of this woman is enough to pose is made explicit when, in *Nadja*, Breton refers to "this veritable Sphinx beneath the features of a charming

[8]

young woman." Identification of the theme of interrogation with that of the role attributable to the marvelous in human life now becomes complete when Breton describes himself as appearing before Nadja "like a man dumbfounded at the feet of the Sphinx."

What, then, is the nature of the question raised by Breton's encounter with the Sphinx? In a footnote to the 1963 edition of *Nadja*, Breton himself wonders what he could have been seeking and, faced with the inconclusiveness of his own text, admits that at the time the book was written surrealism was still seeking its way.

What might be taken for the weakness of Breton's position is really its strength. Breton was a man who, without fear of ridicule, could mention in *Nadja* one of his cherished wishes —that of meeting at night, in a wood, a beautiful naked woman —and then observe, "or rather, such a wish no longer meaning anything, once expressed, I regret to an incredible degree not having encountered her." This was a man who admitted that at one time he would leave open his hotel room door, in the hope of awaking to find by his side a woman he had not chosen. Just as gladly as he would have accepted such a companion, Breton (then thirty years old) accepted Nadja. Concerned with gathering evidence of what the surrealists were already calling "daily magic," Breton could not resist the attraction of this "inspiring creature," whom he found able to release in him that sense of the marvelous to which surrealism attaches so much importance. Without difficulty, he realized that, whatever the nature of the question his meetings with Nadja would answer, he must continue to see her: "And what if I no longer saw her? *I no longer would know.* I would have deserved therefore not to know."

An essential clue to the nature of the knowledge Breton

[9]

aspires to attain through contact with Nadja is provided in his admission, "While close to her I am closer to the things that are close to her." The usefulness of this clue is confirmed by consideration of the function reserved for the photographs reproduced in *Nadja*.

Breton's meetings with Nadja took place in Paris. However, as a study of his text confirms, his aim in utilizing photographs of certain Paris landmarks is not an impression of greater realism. The first sentence of *Nadja* is "Who am I?" Soon Breton is asking "Whom do I haunt?" and reflecting upon the verb *haunt:* "It gives me to understand that what I regard as the objective, more or less deliberate manifestations of my existence are only what passes within the limits of this life from an activity the true extent of which is quite unknown to me." The illustrations in *Nadja* relate to these manifestations. In a foreword written in 1962, Breton spoke of the battle which takes place within man between subjectivity and objectivity, noting that the latter is usually the victor. The incidents reported in *Nadja* appear to mark a welcome reversal of this depressing trend. They are noteworthy instances of privileged insight in which, as Pierre Mabille puts it in his *Le Miroir du Merveilleux*, "an extraordinary complicity is established between the needs of the heart, between the processes of thought and the laws of a universe we wrongly believed to be mechanical, anonymous and indifferent." Such moments constitute the primary material of *Nadja*, whose author's sense of privilege comes from his conviction that, through contact with certain manifestations of objective reality, he can hope to discover the true nature of his own subjectivity: *who* he is.

Nadja rejects the idea of the reconquest of the self, and defends the view that the self exists not in the past but in the future, as a potentiality to be explored, with every chance of infinite progress toward discovery and understanding. Breton shows himself to be less interested in recognition (*reconnaissance*) than in cognition (*connaissance*). He has in view "a general aptitude that would be special to me, and is not given to me." Hence, naturally, the complete uselessness of merely attempting to copy the real with exactitude. Not until one has undertaken a search for more than is given, through the confrontation of the subjective with the objective, can the latter take on its true meaning, as the photographs of *Nadja* take their significance from the emotions associated with them in the text. Accordingly, Breton sees himself as he sees J. K. Huysmans: "the object of those perpetual solicitations which seem to come from without, and to immobilize us for a few seconds before one of those fortuitous arrangements, of a more or less new character, to which it seems that, by thoroughly questioning ourselves, we should find in us the secret."

So, in the final analysis, what Breton finds in his meetings with Nadja is the occasion for self-discovery, as the solution to the riddle of the Sphinx becomes truly man himself. If the answer to human needs comes from within, though, it is not to be found by turning one's back upon reality. This is a major discovery to which *Nadja* testifies. Meeting Nadja constitutes for Breton proof that the marvelous is innate in the real, thus offering support to a theory of immanence according to which "surreality is contained in reality itself, and is neither superior nor exterior to it. And conversely, because the container is also the content. It is almost a matter of communicating vessels between container and content" (*Le Surréalisme et la Peinture*).

Meanwhile, unfortunately, Nadja had been committed to an asylum, leaving Breton with the guilty feeling that perhaps he had not helped her as much as he might have done. The ambiguity of Breton's position cannot escape notice: although genuinely concerned for Nadja's fate, Breton had retained a particular interest in the kind of liberation that madness grants the imagination, ever since he had had occasion to observe insanity during the war while attached to the Second Army Psychiatric Center at St. Dizier. One wonders if his encounter with Nadja did not provide the necessary impetus for the inclusion in *L'Immaculée Conception* (1930) of a section entitled "Les Possessions," offering five essays in simulation of various states of insanity, which the public was asked to judge on their *poetic* merit. Be that as it may, two years later, in November, 1932, appeared *Les Vases communicants* (The Communicating Vessels), which demonstrated what progress in his search for liberation Breton's acquaintance with Nadja had made possible.

Les Vases communicants describes Breton's state of mind in mid-1931. Intellectually, he was feeling acutely the indifference of a public too ready to identify surrealism's defense of revolution with a debased form of romanticism. His frustration was aggravated by a deep sense of emotional disturbance, resulting from the loss of the woman he loved. Breton had reached the point of questioning the vitality of surrealist action. It would be understandable, in the circumstances, if he had turned away from the problems to which surrealism lent urgency, and had fallen back upon some kind of evasion. At first sight, indeed, it would seem that *Les Vases communicants*, concerned as it is with the communicating vessels of dreaming and waking experience, reflects such an inclination to escape and to resort to substitutes. But nothing could be further from the truth than the assumption that *Les Vases communicants* betrays surrealist principles.

Les Vases communicants states clearly Breton's wish to have us understand that surrealism has attempted to "place a conductor between the all too dissociated worlds of waking and dreaming, of external reality and internal reality, of reason and madness, of the calm of knowledge and of love, of life for life's sake and of revolution." Far from relinquishing positions so far gained, Breton intends his new book to move forward from an assertion that is fundamental to surrealist theory: that surrealism is capable of resolving, to the individual's satisfaction, certain antinomies generally regarded as basic to human existence.

As is his custom, Breton faces the problems which command his attention from the standpoint of personal experience. In this instance, he analyzes several of his own dreams, to which incidents occurring in April, 1931, lend special significance. Basing his conclusions upon the postulation that every reader will be struck by the analogy of what he recounts with the dream state, as this is generally conceived, Breton asks us to notice "how strangely the exigency of desire searching for the *object* of its realization arranges the exterior data, selfishly tending to retain of these only that which may serve its cause." The point at issue presents no novelty to those who have noticed how selective are the details supporting the conclusions drawn in *Nadja*. Those unmoved by the surrealist manifestoes or by *Nadja* will be equally indifferent to what *Les Vases communicants* has to say. For now it becomes Breton's intention to present an argument which, "by means of the dream, attempts to prosecute materialist knowledge," taking its point of departure in the conviction that "the world of the dream and the real world are one and the same."

Les Vases communicants maintains the emphasis upon the role of the subjective element in man's pursuit of the exploration of objective reality with the purpose of extending knowledge. It gives a glimpse of the means available to make dreams "serve a

[13]

greater understanding of the dreamer's fundamental aspirations, as well as a more accurate appreciation of his immediate needs." At the same time, categorical dismissal of the idea that man should retreat into dreams in order to escape the pressure of reality allows Breton to stress another aspect of the surrealist program.

In *Les Vases communicants* Breton writes of those who "have considered once and for all that after so many interpretations of the world it was time to go on to its transformation."—The conclusions already reached in *Nadja* about the relationship subjectivity must bear to objectivity lead increasingly, in Breton's subsequent publications, to emphasis upon the need for transforming the latter. The immediate consequences are twofold. On the one hand, Breton publishes *Les Vases communicants* in order to draw attention, through an examination of those processes of the mind on which reflection exercises least influence, to the existence of a "capillary tissue," capable of "ensuring the constant exchange which must take place in thought between the internal and external worlds." On the other hand, he publishes *Position politique du Surréalisme* (1935).

Breton, approaching all matters from the surrealist standpoint, saw no conflict between the privately motivated curiosity which impelled him to write *Les Vases communicants* and a sense of public responsibility which resulted in his delivering the lectures collected in *Position politique du Surréalisme*. The demonstration Breton took it upon himself to provide, in *Les Vases communicants*, of the interpenetration of dream and reality, of the inner and outer worlds, constituted a necessary advance from the *Second Manifesto*, of June, 1930. In this manifesto could be observed the effects of increasing awareness of the social and moral consequences of surrealism's defense of the principle of integral freedom.

[14]

Breton writes in *Les Vases communicants:* "Thus we arrive at conceiving a synthetic attitude in which the need to transform the world radically finds itself reconciled with the need to interpret it as completely as possible." At no time in the history of surrealism has it been possible to question the sincerity of a complementary declaration, which Breton made in 1930 and published in *Point du Jour* (1934): "We persist, here, in wishing to deduce revolutionary duty from the most general human duty, from human duty such as, in the place we occupy, it is given to us to conceive it."

The theoretical positions defended by the surrealists were mapped once again in a lecture Breton gave in Brussels and published under the title *Qu'est-ce que le Surréalisme?* (1934). At the same time the surrealist outlook was defined in two other texts, which Breton wrote with Eluard: *Notes sur la Poésie* (1936), reprinted from the last number of *La Révolution surréaliste* (1929), and the catalogue of the 1938 International Surrealist Exhibition, *Dictionnaire abrégé du Surréalisme.* To those interested in identifying the contribution made by Breton's independent effort to surrealist theory and in understanding his literary personality, the most significant of his publications during the second half of the decade preceding the Second World War was, though, *L'Amour fou.*

In *Point du Jour*, Breton spoke for all the surrealists when he asserted, "There is no solution outside love." Yet after reading in *Les Vases communicants* that love needs to be "rebuilt" and reestablished on its "true basis," one may feel a little disappointed when, in *L'Amour fou,* one comes upon the statement: "Never was there any forbidden fruit. Temptation alone is divine." Does the reinvention of love mean no more than the promotion of sexual freedom, in disdain for moral reprobation?

[15]

Hardly. Breton has in view quite a different form of liberation, for which those who know his *Position politique du Surréalisme* are partly prepared.

Although he does not consider love to be an instrument of political revolt, Breton does see in the repressive forces that oppose the love experience the very social pressures which need to be combated on the political plane, if man is to attain full liberty. In his mind, the right to love and the need to guarantee all men independence of action go together, since both postulate the transformation of the world.

Of necessity, discussion of "mad love" obliges Breton to face the problem of the conflict resulting from the opposition which social conditions offer an individual's love for another. Even so, social protest is not the primary theme of *L'Amour fou*. The demands of love are to be met within the social framework, it is true, but only by "abandoning ordinary logical paths." What calls for explanation, therefore, is the sentence with which Breton brought *Nadja* to a close and which he was to repeat in 1942, in an essay on Max Ernst: "Beauty will be CONVULSIVE or will not exist."

L'Amour fou reveals that the meaning of the adjective "convulsive" is to be sought through an examination of the relationship existing between a person in love and the object of his passion. The presence of convulsive love is guaranteed, Breton claims, by what he calls "circumstantial magic." Hence the care taken in *L'Amour fou* to identify the characteristics Breton feels are attributable to certain unusual circumstances recalled in his book. These circumstances are brought together by the element he regards as their common denominator—desire. In *L'Amour fou* desire is seen to have its own devious, strange ways of seeking out and taking possession of its object. Breton now makes the discovery that "Tournesol," which he wrote in 1923, was a prophetic poem, forecasting events, which did not take place until 1934, that culminated in his marriage with Jacqueline Lamba, the following year. He speaks too of visiting the flea-market with Alberto Giacometti, and of finding a mask and wooden spoon. Then he explains how the mask appeared to "take its place" in Giacometti's personal search (by suggesting the features necessary to complete a sculpture he had been unable to finish), and how the spoon answered some quite unconscious needs of his own.

Throughout *L'Amour fou* we may trace Breton's preoccupation with a familiar question: the problem of the relationship of objectivity to subjectivity. His examination of the question advances a step in *L'Amour fou*, thanks to his increased awareness of the role of chance in human affairs.

Between desire and its objectively represented object stands beneficent chance, to which Breton owed his meeting with Nadja. Chance now seemed to be embodied in found objects (*objets trouvés*), as Breton concluded that the find (*trouvaille*) exercises a remarkable magnetism, because it is capable of revealing in us desires of which we have remained ignorant. A footnote in *L'Amour fou* refers readers to *Les Vases communicants*, as Breton reminds us that the *trouvaille* has the same function as the dream, "in that it liberates the individual from paralyzing affective scruples, comforts him and allows him to understand that the obstacle which he might have believed insurmountable has been passed."

The effect of the *find* is similar to that of the electric storm: lightning is released, and unexpected illumination results. The *trouvaille* induces reconsideration of a question which was of fundamental importance for Breton since his *Introduction au Discours sur le Peu de Réalité* testified to his belief that the merit attaching to objective reality may vary from zero to

[17]

infinity. The *find* that proves to correspond to a desire, previously inarticulate, illuminates reality in a way which Breton considered to be especially revealing. So long as it relates to the individual's inner needs, its role is analogous to that of love, since love sheds light on the real, to the degree that subjective responsiveness to the outside world is conditioned by the emotional experience of passionate attachment. Above all, love is the supreme form of desire, capable of the kind of transformation which the adjective "convulsive" suggests: a violent disturbance takes place that affects the relationship of man to society. Thus the attention given to love in *L'Amour fou* carries forward the inquiry undertaken in Breton's previous essays, as he now asserts that only by adducing evidence of the close connection of the real to the imaginative can one hope to strike a new blow against the unfounded distinction between the subjective and the objective.

In this sense, we may speak of Breton as a writer who used his own experience in order to probe and evaluate problems he felt were significant for all men. He did not examine events isolated from his own life in order to discover what separated him from others, but to uncover what linked his desires with theirs. In *L'Amour fou*, Breton accumulated proof of "irrationality close at hand," basing his evidence upon the experience he was best able to record with fidelity—his own. He expressed continued confidence in the rewards obtainable by unwavering willingness to accept all that chance may place in one's path: "Indépendamment de ce qui arrive, n'arrive pas, c'est l'attente qui est magnifique." It is characteristic of Breton that he should use the word *attente* here simultaneously as "waiting" and "expectation."

Each of the essays written before the Second World War is intended to assume the significance of a human document, as Breton used the term: testimony to human aspirations which

stand outside the materialistic world. Each essay reveals Breton
to be attentive to what he termed "the beginning of a contact,
dazzling above all, between man and the world of things," and
confirms his interest in defining "the law governing these
mysterious exchanges between the material and the mental."
In stressing on every occasion the revelatory nature of the incidents that claimed his attention, he sought justification for the
statement made in *L'Amour fou:* "The greatest weakness of
contemporary thought seems to me to reside in the extravagant
overestimation of the known compared with what remains to
be known."

In 1939 Breton was recalled to military service. The collapse
of the French Army occurred when Breton was in the Free
Zone. There he was demobilized in 1940, and wrote the long
poem "Fata Morgana," as well as his *Anthologie de l'Humour
noir.* Finally, he made his way in the following year via Martinique to the United States.

Breton's period of residence in the United States was marked
by two important statements on surrealism: a lecture delivered
at Yale University in 1942, "Situation du Surréalisme entre les
deux Guerres," and "Prolégomènes à un Troisième Manifeste
du Surréalisme ou Non" (1942). From this period dates also the
essay *Arcane 17*, which appeared in New York two years later.

No one could blame Breton if *Arcane 17* displayed some concern for pressing personal problems. Stress of circumstance—
his exile from France at the time when news reports told of the
Allies' advance upon Paris—might have led him excusably to give
his essay an orientation and an emphasis which would seem,
today, dated. However, far from being outmoded, *Arcane 17*
marks the culmination of certain themes which run through the
essays written during the twenties and thirties.

A framework for *Arcane 17* is provided by the logbook of a trip made off the Gaspé Peninsula in 1944. It is true that the thoughts accompanying descriptive passages evoking the Gulf of St. Lawrence find their point of departure in the news of the Allies' advance through France. But, typically, when raising the question of "resistance" and "liberation," Breton rejects the popular interpretations placed on these words in Occupied France, and chooses to discuss freedom and rebellion in relation neither to private nor to national destiny. Faithful to the principles that have governed his life for two decades, he undertakes to evaluate man's situation in the perspective which surrealism recommends.

Breton gives attention to those permanent elements of civilization which remain untouched by such disruptive circumstances as war brings. Among the constants that must be acknowledged in man's thought Breton gives prominence to the aspiration toward freedom. This is not merely freedom from alien domination but a permanent state of rebellion which, he claims, "carries its justification within itself, quite independently of the chance it has of modifying or not modifying the state of affairs that determines it."

So far as Breton was concerned, recent events in France proved conclusively that liberation is a meaningless concept so long as it implies anything less than "a dynamic state." This is why, in *Arcane 17*, he admits to being dissatisfied when he provisionally defines liberty "by opposition to all forms of servitude and constraint." Such a definition, he argues, tends to represent liberty as a state—"that is to say in immobility." And this, he declares, anticipating intuitively the conclusions to which the spectacle of postwar France would bring him in *La Lampe dans l'Horloge* (1948), leads inevitably to its ruination. Man's aspirations toward liberty, on the contrary, should be

[20]

able to "re-create themselves ceaselessly." This means that liberty must be conceived not as a state but as "a *vital force*," entailing "a continual progression": liberty stands for the affirmation of what man can be, rather than of what he is.

Arcane 17 expands conclusions earlier expressed in *L'Amour fou*, which amply demonstrated the incompatibility of social demands and the full development and satisfaction of human desire. Basically, poetry and love are, in Breton's eyes, antisocial activities, interrelated assertions of a principle of liberty much farther-reaching in its effects than the postulation of political self-determination alone would entail. Love, poetry, and art are presented in *Arcane 17* as the principal means by which man's confidence can be renewed and by which his thought can be enabled to "take to the open sea once again."

It is therefore entirely appropriate that throughout *Arcane 17* runs the lyrical theme of Breton's love for Elisa, whom he met in 1943 and married in 1945. Love nourishes protest against what Breton calls "opacity" and considers to be man's greatest enemy, because it is the product of inculcated respect for conventional opinions. Beyond question, his attachment to Elisa reinforced Breton's belief in love, "the true panacea," as solely capable of fusing existence and essence in complete harmony. And so in *Arcane 17* may be detected the growing influence of Fourier. Breton's insistence upon words like "panacea" and "regeneration" indicate that he turns to love for something other than an example of passion untrammeled by social controls. Woman finally reaches her full stature in Breton's writing as, rejecting the idea of Christian redemption, he asks of love the solution to man's most serious problems: "The great malediction is raised, and it is in human love that all the regenerative power of the world resides."

Now Breton gives prominence to a profoundly surrealist

theme as he casts woman in the role of mediatrix. Breton shows woman releasing man from opacity, as he once more evokes the figure of Melusina, taking care to emphasize that he does not intend the "child-woman" to be esteemed in opposition to mature woman. In Melusina seems to reside "in a state of absolute transparency the *other* prism of vision which we obstinately refuse to take into account, because it obeys very different laws which masculine despotism must prevent at all cost from being divulged."

Convinced that man's thinking has brought nothing but suffering, Breton is persuaded that it is time to look at last to woman for guidance. He sees Melusina as "always woman lost, the one who sings to the imagination of man, but, after what trials for her and for him, she must also be woman found once more." He judges her to be perpetually attractive to poets since, as child-woman, she is able to dissipate the best-organized systems: "Nothing has been able to make her subject to them or understood by them."

Breton's admiration for Melusina is completely consistent with his conviction that it is imperative to release human life and thought from the oppressive weight of time. She represents the very personification of revolt and liberty as, synthesizing the themes of his essay, Breton brings it to a close with a passage in which his calm confidence in the vitality of the principle of liberty finds full expression: "It is revolt itself, revolt alone that is creative of light. And this light can know only three paths: poetry, liberty, and love which must inspire the same ardor and converge, so as to make of it the very cup of eternal youth, on the darker and most illuminable point of the human heart."

Those who persist in defending the view that surrealism's period of activity was confined to the years between the two

[22]

world wars believe themselves entitled to draw support from two facts at least. First, it is clear that, thanks to the dispersion of the French surrealist group in 1940 and the absence of its major figures during the Occupation, by 1945 surrealism had lost the initiative in France. Breton returned to Paris in 1946 to find that the existentialism of Jean-Paul Sartre now commanded the attention of French youth. Despite a major international surrealist exhibition in Paris in 1947, it was several years before distracting considerations like the surrealists' abstention from participation in the Resistance ceased to cloud judgment upon the contribution surrealism continued to be capable of making. Second, after the war the fortunes of the elder surrealists entered a new phase. These writers, who in the past so often had had to publish privately, now found their work being reprinted by commercial houses. Surrealism was achieving a form of consecration which was not to be entirely advantageous, since it tended to assume the character of an interment.

In the case of André Breton, especially, the reprinting of the *Manifestoes* in 1946 and of *Arcane 17* in 1947, together with the appearance of a representative selection of his *Poèmes* (1948), appeared to lend credence to the view that here was a writer who had outlived his productive period. *Ode à Charles Fourier* (written in 1945), it is true, was published in 1947, while two other poetic texts, both privately printed, have appeared since. But the twenty years following his return to France would have offered little proof of active interest in the ideas he had defended for so long had Breton not made an impressive contribution as an art critic.

It may be tempting to see in the author of *L'Art magique* (1957), written with the help of Gérard Legrand, of the "prose parallels" which accompanied Miró's *Constellations* in 1959, and above all of the greatly expanded edition of *Le Surréalisme et la Peinture* (1965) a writer whose critical personality set him apart from the person to whom we owe some of the most significant of the surrealist essays. In reality, one would be guilty of a grave misunderstanding in doing so, since Breton himself made no distinction between those of his writings in which he explored the meaning of his own life and those in which he examined pictorial evidence of the experience of others. His observations on art confirm attitudes expressed in his essays, and complete our understanding of his outlook.

In July, 1938, the question of the relationship of art to politics, which *Position politique du Surréalisme* had shown three years before to have its roots in Breton's deep concern for the revolutionary role of art, was posed with the greatest clarity in a manifesto, *Pour un Art révolutionnaire indépendant*, which Breton wrote in collaboration with Leon Trotsky, during a visit to Mexico. That same year Breton praised Frida Kahlo de Rivera because her painting seemed to "stand at the point of intersection of the political (philosophical) line and the artistic line, from which we wish that these lines become unified in one revolutionary consciousness, without, for that reason, the essentially different motives which belong to them being merged." In the following year, in a note on André Masson, Breton assured his readers that the surrealists continued to believe that art must be above all "love rather than hate or pity," insisting that "the problem is no longer as it used to be that of knowing whether a picture 'stands up' for example in a corn field, but if it stands up next to a daily newspaper, open or closed, which is a jungle."

At no time do Breton's articles on painting neglect to stress the need for a "revision of values" and the necessity to measure the appropriateness of artistic means to this end. Breton questions the usefulness of the work of any painter whose eye "limits itself to the passive role of a mirror," and, in a text on Arshile Gorky, asserts in 1945 that the painter's eye is capable of serving as a *fil conducteur* between things apparently unrelated. This return to the image of the clew and of the conductor, familiar to those who have read *Les Vases communicants* and the poem "Vigilance" (1932), is proof enough of consistency in Breton's thought and of his conviction, so clearly imaged in the 1928 version of *Le Surréalisme et la Peinture*, that it is a grave mistake to equate art with imitation.

Breton advises that we replace the exterior model with an interior model, "resolutely giving representation precedence over perception," on the understanding that "nothing around us is object to us, all is subject." So it is that discussion of artists and of their techniques is the occasion for emphasis once again upon the fact that the true object of discussion is reality itself. Speaking of the sculpture of Maria, Breton reaffirms in 1947 what Nadja had taught him: "It is, one can never repeat often enough, the universe that must be interrogated first about man, and not man about the universe."

If Breton's art criticism could provide no more than confirmation of what we have learned already, it would hardly be worth mentioning. It happens, though, that his observations on painting are guaranteed special value by the contribution they make to explaining his poetry.

Unfortunately, reference to the language of painting is such a commonplace of critical jargon that one might easily fail to notice, at first contact with Breton's articles, that he really does consider painting to be a language. Inattention to this fact results in concealment of another, which must be taken into account before we can appreciate how indicative are these writings on art of the attitude Breton adopts toward poetry.

[25]

For him, poetry and painting are truly but two forms of one and the same language, placed at the disposal of those inspired to surrealist expression. Opening the 1928 version of *Le Surréalisme et la Peinture*, we encounter characteristic references to the technique of pictorial automatism as the vehicle which allows Matta, Esteban Frances, and Onslow-Ford to set out to conquer "a new morphology that will exhaust in the most concrete language the whole process by which the psychic has its echo in the physical." Speaking of the work of Tanguy, Breton talks of "sensorial verbs," which he claims "demand not to be conjugated like others," adding: "To this necessity astonishing participles make their response: already seen, already heard, never seen, etc." Breton concludes characteristically: "To see, to hear is nothing. To recognize (or not to recognize) is everything. Between what I recognize and what I do not recognize is I."

We can be sure, of course, that, being in the beginning less confident of the suitability of painting than of poetry to surrealism's aims, Breton was inclined at first to seek as many points of contact as possible between the two media, to bring them closer together by treating the former as he would the latter. But it is evident too that, as the years went by, Breton became convinced of his right to make the same demands upon the painter as upon the poet. By 1939, he could describe the work of Masson as "plastic metaphor in its pure state," and insist, "I mean literarily untranslatable." In an essay on recent trends in surrealist painting, written the same year, he returned to the case of Yves Tanguy to describe the elements typical of his painting as "the words of a language which we do not yet understand, but which soon we shall read and speak, about which we are going to discover that it is the language best suited to new exchanges." A note on Rufino Tamayo, dating from 1950, makes explicit what is hinted here, when Breton admits to his concern for painting as "universal language." We are reminded of his remark, dating from 1928, to the effect that, in the collages of Max Ernst, disparate elements are "seeking to discover for themselves new affinities." We are reminded too of his comment on Joan Miró: "No one comes close to associating as he does the unassociable, to breaking without discrimination that which we do not dare to wish to see broken." Breton consistently gives his trust to those painters in whose work "the key to the mental prison can be found only in breaking those paltry means of cognition: it lies in the free, unlimited play of *analogies*."

Once alerted to Breton's practice of estimating the efficacy of the language of painting as he does that of poetry, we can detect in his art criticism many indications which help to set his approach to poetry in perspective. Identifying the "great enigma"—the permanent cause of the conflict between man and the world—as the "impossibility of justifying everything by the logical," he asks, "How can one call to account the artist, the man of science, for the voices chosen for its satisfaction by the imperious human need to form *against* exterior things other exterior things, in which all the resistance offered by the inner being is at once abdicated and included?" Implied here is "the proposal of an absolutely virgin visual organization," which Breton saw early in his career as corresponding, in the Ernst collages of 1920, to what Lautréamont and Rimbaud desired in poetry: "The exterior object broke with its habitual field of action, its constituent parts became so to speak emancipated, in such a way as to bear with other elements entirely new relationships, escaping the principle of reality but nevertheless having consequences on the plane of the real (upsetting the notion of relationship)." Hence the celebrated maxim: "It is thus impossible for me to consider a picture otherwise than as a window about which my first concern is to know what it looks out upon."

Works of art, Breton believed, should resemble the poems Apollinaire wrote just before the First World War; each should be "an event." Art must draw its justification, he remarked in 1939, "solely from its revelatory power." Almost twenty years later, he reaffirmed in 1958 his preference for painting that seeks to be "a re-creation of the world in terms of the inner necessity experienced by the artist." Thus all that Breton ever wrote about painting and poetry is designed to marshal evidence in support of two statements made in *Le Surréalisme et la Peinture* in 1928: "The essential discovery of surrealism is, in fact, that, without preconceived intention, the pen which runs in writing, or the pencil which runs in drawing, spins an infinitely precious substance of which not all perhaps is material for exchange but which, at least, appears charged with what the poet or painter then has within him by way of emotion." But, Breton urges us to notice, once the stage of emotion for emotion's sake is passed, we should not forget that "at this period, it is reality itself that is at stake." Close attention to the verse he wrote persuades us that, when he spoke of the dream of Max Ernst as "a dream of *mediation*," Breton was identifying in the painter an ambition which gave direction to his own effort in poetry.

In 1919 Breton began to give attention to the phrases which, without his knowing why, would run through his head just before he fell asleep. These phrases, which impressed him by their striking imagery yet syntactical correctness, seemed to be "poetic elements of the first order." The careful consideration they commanded from Breton is to be explained by his state of mind at the time. As he later explained in his first surrealist manifesto: "At that time I had just attempted the poetic adventure with the minimum of luck, that is my aspirations were the same as today. But I had faith in slowness of elaboration to save me from useless contacts, from contacts which I disapproved of greatly." When he was writing the final poems of his first verse collection, *Mont de Piété* (1919), Breton's youthful faith in deliberation, his effort to exploit the interplay of words and the spaces surrounding them on the page—the associations they were capable of stimulating—led him (to take but one example) to spend six months writing a poem, "Forêt-noire," only thirty words long. At this period his method still owed much to the example of Mallarmé. However, this example was ceasing to give promise of the kind of success that by now Breton was seeking. Hence his decision to undertake with Philippe Soupault to reproduce, by the deliberate exclusion of all extraneous thoughts and ideas, the state in which the proximity of sleep released new and exciting poetic elements. The immediate result was the series of texts published as *Les Champs magnétiques*, reprinted in book form from *Littérature* in 1920. The long-term consequences were to be estimated only when, after he and Soupault had baptized their method *surréalisme* out of respect for Apollinaire, Breton proceeded to write his *Manifeste du Surréalisme*, and to consider the implications of automatism, thanks to which the poet's function becomes that of "modest recording machine."

When, as Breton did, the poet holds literature in contempt, when, distinguishing poetic accomplishment from the practice of literature, he seeks in poetry a valid solution to the problems of human existence, he can feel only indifference for verse in which is to be detected the cardinal sin of care for form. Breton saw form as external to poetry always an unwelcome limitation —through rhyme, rhythm, or whatever other restrictive device

[29]

—upon poetic content. Just as he tired of imitating Mallarmé, so he very soon divested himself of his admiration for Valéry, in accordance with his growing belief that precedence over every other consideration must be given the attainment and presentation of what he called poetic intuition.

Breton subscribed without question to the opinion that poetic excellence can only be the result of spontaneity. To be a poet, in his opinion, is to be the privileged beneficiary of insights which it must be the poet's duty to capture in words. Hence his eagerness to examine the revelations made possible by the exercise of the technique of automatic writing.

The well-known definition supplied in the first surrealist manifesto introduced surrealism as "pure psychic automatism by which we propose to express, either verbally, or in writing, or in any other manner the real function of thought," and presented automatic expression as "thought dictated in the absence of all control exercised by reason." Only too ready to demonstrate the weakness inherent in the postulations upon which surrealism rests, and to show how unsound is the declaration that surrealism stands on "the belief in the superior reality of certain forms of association heretofore neglected, in the omnipotence of the dream, in the disinterested play of thought," critics are generally so busy telling one another that surrealist poetry is not feasible that they have little or no time to notice that this poetry exists, and that Breton was one of its leading practitioners.

Typically, literary critics take pains to dismiss the validity of automatism as a poetic method without admitting that none of them has been able to judge with greater penetration than André Breton the weaknesses inherent in the automatic method. They would do well to note that, although admitting that automatism must produce its share of "dross," Breton never repudiated its contribution to his own poetry. A letter addressed to Jean Gaulmier establishes his position with clarity: "I take care not to reread the texts of *Poisson soluble*, no doubt because the manner in which they were obtained prevents my passing calm judgment upon them, because 'looked at coolly' they would soon overwhelm me with their weaknesses—which, deep down, does not stop me from remaining *jealously faithful to the spirit that controls them*." This spirit counts far more than the results first obtained by the exercise of automatism. In this sense, therefore, Julien Gracq very properly stressed the value of *Poisson soluble* when he spoke of its contents as "poems that are an invitation to poetry." The technique to which *Poisson soluble* owes its existence is one that redefined poetry at a time when, discouraged with results obtained by imitation of other poets, Breton was seeking a poetic mode promising satisfaction of increasingly urgent needs.

What is important for us is not so much assessment of the first texts which Breton owed to automatism, as appreciation of the fact that the automatic method opened up perspectives where, previously, the prospect had seemed depressingly uninviting. Initiated by automatic practice, Breton was to be confirmed in his belief that innovation in poetic language was an imminent possibility as well as a pressing necessity.

Here we see the reason for a striking change in language that becomes noticeable when, turning from his prose works, one begins to read Breton's poetry. It is apparent that, once he came to write verse, he willingly abandoned the remarkably persuasive style which distinguishes his prose. The author to whom we are indebted for *Arcane 17* is also the writer who once declared that the function of language is not to communicate, and who was to make public his lack of concern for that elementary characteristic of language, its "power of immediate exchange."

[31]

In his *Introduction au Discours sur le Peu de Réalité*, Breton invites us to address our critical faculties to the laws presiding over verbal arrangements and asks, "Does not the mediocrity of our universe depend upon our power of enunciation?"

The special power he attributed to poetic enunciation accounts for Breton's sharp reproval of all who purport to *explain* the poetic image. As early as September, 1924, his *Introduction au Discours* dismissed as impertinent explanations provided in a recent anthology: "What Saint-Pol-Roux wished to say," he proclaimed, "you can be sure he said." The pretension of the language of reason to elucidate that of poetry is something to which Breton's instincts commanded resistance. Meanwhile, in his own poetry, linguistic experimentation, whatever degree of unconscious motivation is involved in its use, is an expression of revolt against a universe that has ceased to accord with man's desires. Hence his unyielding resistance to attempts that may be made to explain the results such experimentation brings. The poetic image, as he assessed its vitality, does not only deny explanation; it defies it. "Let us not forget," he warned, "that only a certain practical necessity prevents us from granting poetic testimony a value equal to that granted, for example, the testimony of an explorer." Undermining practical necessity, Breton the poet reserved for himself the role, rights, and privileges of an explorer.

To the extent that the practice of poetry becomes an exploratory venture, the pleasure it provides is that of the *trouvaille*, which plays the same part in a Breton poem as found objects do in the events discussed in *L'Amour fou*. In both cases the *find* expresses concretely the externalization of desires, and assumes consequently the value of revelation, to become the "marvelous precipitate of desire," capable of enlarging the universe. This surely is why an article entitled "Les Mots sans Rides" (Words without Wrinkles), reprinted in *Les Pas perdus*, spoke out boldly for innovation in poetic language and pointed to the striking verbal effects for which Robert Desnos and Marcel Duchamp were responsible. Breton might have cited just as pertinently other young poets, first associated with dada and then affiliated with surrealism, who were expressing their opposition to literary forms they regarded as outdated through iconoclastic humor, anti-aesthetic images, vulgarity, and mocking word-play. Yet, during the period when Desnos was at work on *Rrose Sélavy*, *L'Aumonyme*, and *Langage cuit*, when Roger Vitrac was preparing *Peau-Asie*, and Paul Eluard was engaged in composing his *Exemples*, Breton himself was writing less revolutionary poetic texts: *Clair de Terre*.

When reading *Clair de Terre*, published in 1923, we comprehend that of all the young surrealists Breton had most need to liberate himself from early literary influences. Today the poems in this volume appear self-conscious, contrived, and generally lacking in the spontaneity their author was soon to advocate. Breton was inclined still to rely on conventional comparisons and somewhat labored grammatical constructions. As yet, certainly, his use of phrases built upon the word *comme* gave no foretaste of the contribution later to be demanded of *like* once he had come to the conclusion that it has the same grammatical function as a verb, being possessed of the capacity to make something happen between the words it brings together.

Clair de Terre, of course, antedated the first surrealist manifesto. Before Breton could find his way as a poet, it remained for him to discover that "language has been given man so that he may make surrealist use of it." Soon, however, two volumes of poetry which he helped to write in 1930 (*Ralentir Travaux* and *L'Immaculée Conception*) bore witness to his eagerness to

[33]

test the surrealist capabilities of language. Then in 1931 his poem "L'Union libre," published anonymously under the imprint Editions surréalistes, inaugurated a period of poetic productivity marked by the publication of *Le Revolver à Cheveux blancs* (1932) and *L'Air de l'Eau* (1934).

By highlighting the constant exchange taking place in thought between "the internal and external worlds," and by emphasizing that the demands of love are to be met by "abandoning ordinary logical paths," *Les Vases communicants* indicated the theoretical basis upon which the poem "L'Union libre" was built.

In "L'Union libre" a succession of images displayed in their arrangement no more order than might be expected from the freely associative method to which they owe their existence and presentation. Clearly, justification for the poetic method utilized in this poem is not to be found in the realm of the logical and the rational. We must refer, for an understanding of this text, to *Les Vases communicants*, where Breton writes: "The spirit is marvelously prompt to seize the faintest rapport that can exist between two objects selected by chance and the poets know they can always, without fear of deceit, say that the one is *like* the other: the only hierarchy that may be established among poets can rest solely upon the greater or lesser liberty which they demonstrate in this respect." A footnote clarifies: "To compare two subjects as distant as possible one from the other, or, by any other method, to bring them face to face, remains the highest task to which poetry can aspire."

Reading "L'Union libre" we see how this conception of poetry leads in Breton's verse, through circumstantial magic and the creation of convulsive beauty, to the formulation of the exigency of desire, working analogously to the dream in its search for "the *object* of its realization" in such a way as to "arrange" the exterior data borrowed from objective reality. The clew in "L'Union libre" is the poet's love for his wife, which provides the contact between him and the world of things, in such a manner as to make explicit Breton's meaning when he declared that nothing around us is object; all is subject. The result is a text drawing its strength from *l'amour fou*, and typical of Breton's surrealist poetry in its most striking form. One arresting image ("My wife with the tongue of a stabbed host") is set off by a line of disarming banality ("With the tongue of a doll that opens and closes its eyes"). Then the latter verse, in which the poetic charge is low, appears to suggest other lines which do not occur until later in the poem, as Breton speaks of "the movement of clockwork and despair" and writes:

> My wife with hips of a skiff
> With hips of luster and of arrow-feathers
> And of shafts of white peacock plumes
> Of imperceptible swaying.

If admissible at all, relationships of this kind between individual verses have to be established by the reader himself. Given the method of "free union" thanks to which the images accumulate, there can be no question of demanding of the poet a deliberate pattern of imagery. "L'Union libre" is the product of a hypnotic state, in which the invocation of automatism is instinctive. Taking as an example the verse "Ma femme aux mollets de moelle de sureau" (My wife with calves of elder pith), we notice how an obscure relationship exists audibly between *mollets* and *moelle*, even though it is not rationally explicable. The result is a line in which sound association of the kind first practiced by Raymond Roussel produces a statement which, however reprehensible rationally, articulates a desire to which Breton's *Introduction au Discours sur le Peu de Réalité* has confessed: "The idea of a bed of stones or of feathers is equally unbearable to me: What do you expect; I can sleep only on a bed of elder pith."

It is worth pausing here, because the verse quoted above exemplifies an essential feature of Breton's poetic art. Echoing Apollinaire's maxim, he asserts in *L'Amour fou:* "Surprise must be sought for itself, unconditionally." Surprise, for Breton, exists "in the intrication in a single object of the natural and the supernatural, in the emotion of holding the lyre-bird and at the same time feeling it escape." To those who read hurriedly, these words might seem to authorize the very kind of verbal contrivance which Breton abjured, once the potentiality of surrealism was revealed to him. In reality, Breton is expressing his confidence in the ability of language to surprise the poet himself, before it surprises his readers. He is referring to the verbal *trouvaille,* which has the effect of bringing to the poet's attention, with the shock of surprise, elements of his own thought and feeling, previously imprisoned within the unconscious.

There seems no reason to doubt that here we touch upon the reason which provoked protest from Breton in an article reprinted in *La Clé des Champs* (1953) directed against those who qualify poets as visionaries: "The great poets are 'auditives' not visionaries. In them vision, the 'illumination,' is, in any case, not the *cause* but the *effect*." While this observation embodies a tendentious definition of poetry, it does indicate both the nature of the ambition Breton had as a poet and the method by which he sought to fulfill it. When, during a lecture in Prague on March 29, 1935, he followed Hegel's lead in placing poetry above all the other arts as the only universal art, he cited also Lautréamont, borrowing as the surrealists frequently do the phrase "poetry must be made by all," and adding *"poetry must be heard by all."*

The gravity which has contributed to make Breton one of the most remarkable prose stylists France has known in this century ruled out, from the beginning, all possibility of levity in his verse. One misses the joyous destructiveness which gave the early verse of Aragon its brilliance, just as one misses the inner turbulence which left its mark on the poems of Antonin Artaud. Time has confirmed the conclusion which in the twenties might have seemed premature; Breton's poetic tone takes its place between the violence of Péret's and the artful simplicity of Eluard's.

As a poet, Breton spoke with authoritative tones. So much so, indeed, that a malicious observer might be inclined to attribute special importance to his respect for Victor Hugo. From the moment when Breton's poetry began to evidence self-assurance, it was characterized by a tone which has done much to lend support to accusations that he assumed the role of pontiff. Breton's unshakable conviction that his was a privileged voice underlies many of his statements which lend themselves to misinterpretation. It is displayed even better in an innate respect for language patterns and an intuitive command of their capabilities. These qualities would strike a discordant note of harmony in the calculated cacophony of early surrealist writing were it not that Breton possessed to an uncanny degree the power to persuade us that mediation is, in his case, not a self-imposed role but a natural gift. In a way that sets his verse notably apart from his companions' in the surrealist venture, Breton undertook to give language in his poetry the function surrealism attributes to it: "to make cognition take a long step." In a manner totally consistent with the preoccupations which provide his essays with their dominant themes, he sought to face the fundamental problem of perception and representation, observing attentively, along the way, how words "make love."

In 1932 "L'Union libre" was followed by Breton's first collection of truly surrealist verse, *Le Revolver à Cheveux blancs* (The White-haired Revolver). Breton prefaced this volume with the unequivocal statement, "Imagination is not a gift but an object of conquest par excellence." He declared too that it does not have to "humiliate itself before life" because the imaginary is "that which tends to become real." Anyone who questions Breton's firm belief in this surrealist-inspired principle will neither understand his poetry nor comprehend why it was written.

In the poems of *Le Revolver à Cheveux blancs* confidence in the ultimate supremacy of the subjective over the objective finds clear expression. We are introduced to a universe created by the exercise of poetic imagination of a remarkable nature. This is a universe of anticipated and wished-for experience, in which Breton never once doubts that his role is that of revelator. Reconciliation of desire with the world of reality is shown to be an act of conquest, not of resigned acceptance, as the poet becomes an explorer who seeks and finds "more than is given." Like the eye of the painter Arshile Gorky, praised by Breton for providing a *fil conducteur* between things apparently unconnected with one another, the imagination of the poet supplies a guiding thread through the labyrinthine ways of the unforeseen and the hoped-for. In such a universe as the imagination brings within his purview, chronological time is among the first elements of the rational world to lose their power. Present and future exist contemporaneously because no distinction need be made any longer between what is and what the imagination gives assurances will be. Dismissal of clock time is thus a token of the ever-widening influence of the imagined, tending progressively to take the place of the real. Absence of time sequence is the prophetic sign of the metamorphosis of reality in response to the imperious command of desire.

In the fluid time vacuum of Breton's poetry, we are conscious of flux, of a world changing so rapidly that we barely have the opportunity to identify an object before it is transformed into another with such facility as to dispose of any preconceptions we may retain regarding an ordered world.

Of each of his poems of *Le Revolver à Cheveux blancs* Breton might say, as he does of one of them, that they represent a descent "à l'intérieur de ma pensée." Thought, here, is naturally not reasoned observation. Rather it is an intuitive exploration of feelings and aspiration made possible only when the poet, having discovered that "the bars are on the inside of the cage," has found a way to prize them apart and to escape inward, often under the enticement of a vision of feminine beauty, half-Ariadne, half-Melusina. Now he comes to see that all the external manifestations we call real are but the elements from which the imagination must and will reconstruct the world. Acknowledging no outside authority, "caretaker" of a world that no one has seen before, he enjoys the liberty to "chase away before [him] real appearances." Absence and presence are "in connivance," as he expresses his revolt against the "consent" which the rational world extorts.

Like those of *Le Revolver*, the poems of *L'Air de l'Eau*, which succeeded them in 1934, record moments in which the façade of the real crumbles to uncover the surreal. They offer examples of prescience of a kind that disposes of the "great interdiction" which Breton is sure that poetry can remove. On the voyage of discovery that is the poem, Breton sees things that can be rendered only in a language which ignores the ordered classifications of a world all too familiar. Here a woman passes "with the sound of flowers," there female singing voices "have the color of sand on tender and dangerous shores." Phrases of this type, and the texts from which they come, project the theory of immanence upon which Breton's surrealism rests, attesting the vision that is granted man once "the bars of the spectacle are twisted marvelously," and he becomes aware of the splitting of "the frightful mental milestones."

The impact of the poet's vision of enfranchisement is not diminished by its brevity. On the contrary, the excitement communicated in a poem like "Au beau demi-jour de 1934" comes largely from the intensity of Breton's sense of release accompanied by the realization that conventional reality presents the constant menace of effacing what has been glimpsed momentarily. The more we read his verse, the more we perceive that it is the fugacity of the imaginative revelation and its fragility which give his poetry its special mood. These elements take their effect in conjunction with the poet's expressions of joy at having been the recipient of a revelation for which there is no substitute in the world of day-to-day reality. What he stresses above all is the privilege of penetrating appearances: "I have only a transparent body," he writes, "within which transparent doves hurl themselves upon a transparent dagger held by a transparent hand." Divesting himself of the constrictive feeling of the duality of body and soul, he animates a universe all his own: "*I* am the unreal breath of this garden."

Even more than in *Le Revolver*, Breton associates his sense of penetration in *L'Air de l'Eau* with the experience of love. Woman is at once mediatrix and initiatrix as, anticipating the prose texts of *L'Amour fou*, new poems celebrate in love "this rushing together of systems considered separately as subjective" which

> Sets off a series of very real phenomena
> That take part in the formation of a distinct world
> Of a kind to bring shame on what we would perceive
> Without it.

Such is the wonder released in the poet, such his excitement at the spectacle of a new world which shames the old, that we cannot expect him to express his feelings in language elaborated for use in the world he delights in leaving behind. Breton's is the language of the new, a lyricism nurtured by the creative play of analogies, as he sings of "marvelous infiltrations" which, no longer content to exist side by side with the conventional, in the end replace it altogether.

Here should be noted the place reserved in Breton's poetry for coincidence, the coming together of the imagined with the real, in a manner similar to that of the collages of Ernst, which Ernst himself defined as "the coupling of two realities, irreconcilable in appearance, upon a plane which apparently does not suit them." Where Ernst speaks of the coupling of disparate realities, Breton talks of words that make love. For both artists the ambition is the same: the invocation of the generative principle, so that something new can be born. This is why in his poem "Fata Morgana" (1940) Breton calls coincidences "veritable beacons in the night of meaning" and love "that promise which goes beyond our comprehension."

After "Fata Morgana" Breton wrote the long poem *Ode à Charles Fourier*, during a period of travel which permitted him to see Nevada, Arizona, and New Mexico, and to come into contact with the Pueblo Indians. Until 1940 Fourier had interested Breton simply from the point of view of social reform. Now, taking with him on his journey west five volumes of Fourier's works, viewing current events from the standpoint which enabled him to write *Arcane 17*, Breton turned away from the horror of the world about him to affirm his hope in the future of mankind, predicted by the nineteenth-century utopists. Among these he was particularly impressed by Fourier, who foresaw the reign of harmony: "I salute you from the Petrified Forest of human culture/ Where nothing is standing any more." The instability of the modern world does nothing to shake Breton's confidence. On the contrary, *Ode à Charles Fourier* affirms his belief that, if the improvement of man's destiny will be effected slowly, "the real lever nevertheless will remain irrational belief in advance toward an Edenic future."

Ode à Charles Fourier was Breton's last major poetic work. So dramatic is the change noticeable in the form and content of the *Ode* that its publication raises questions which cannot be ignored. Does Breton's return to a more conventional poetic form give proof of dissatisfaction with the modes he had practiced for twenty years, in defiance of conventionality? Does his surrender of the opportunity for further discoveries released in coincidences by the use of verbal automatism constitute an admission of failure, which should be taken into account when an estimate is made of his achievements in *Le Revolver à Cheveux blancs* and *L'Air de l'Eau*?

Ode à Charles Fourier stands alone in Breton's work as a philosophical poem. Its origins, examined in detail by Jean Gaulmier, need not be recalled here. We know, from Breton's own statements during an interview with Aimé Patri in March, 1948, that the poem took its point of departure in automatism, finding its unity in the personality of Fourier and in his work, "the greatest constructive work ever elaborated on the basis of unrestrained desire." While apparently seeming to indulge in occasional verse, Breton proposed to "kill" occasional verse. And so in a letter to Gaulmier, dating from 1957, he indicated that his intention in writing his ode was partly critical. He added: "I permitted myself the luxury of an infraction of my own principles (to affranchise poetry at all cost from the controls that feed upon it) and I wished to give this infraction of my own principles the meaning of voluntary elective sacrifice to the memory of Fourier, the most recent person who seemed to be worthy of it."

Just as this letter is a tribute to its author's admiration for Fourier, so it is equally an acknowledgment of continued respect for automatism, which, Gérald Schaeffer has demonstrated, makes a noteworthy contribution to *Ode à Charles Fourier*.

Despite Breton's deliberate control of automatism in his ode, we may detect in it characteristic features which owe their presence in his verse to the poet's search for a universal language. Such a language, Breton maintains, does not have to satisfy the requirements of reason. It bypasses these so as to set off resonances at levels of sensibility, common to all, where reason does not make its influence felt. Breton's central assumption is that the inner demands to which the poet must be responsive at all times, although personal to him, are universal in significance: in seeking the "key to the mental prison," to escape the "principle of reality," he is impelled by his "dream of mediation" to make available to all men the means to liberate themselves.

Escape takes the form of a new understanding of how the external world relates to subjective desire. We witness the substitution by analogy for the explanations of causality of "the spontaneous, extra-lucid, insolent relationship which is established in certain conditions between this thing and that, which common sense would prevent us from bringing face to face." Thus the poet has to be above all the "master of the image," because the image is "the generative element par excellence of that world which in place of the old we intend to make our own."

Here lies Breton's justification for rejecting literary modes which he considers serve no better purpose than to impose on the spirit a discipline inappropriate to it. Only the image, he observes, "gives me the measure of possible liberation, and this liberation is so complete that it frightens me." In the use of the poetic image man takes possession of a power that is proof against all resistance.

"In the final analysis," Breton comments, "everything depends upon our power of voluntary hallucination." The fascinating spectacle of the freedom granted by states which the reasoning world qualifies as insane gives the word "hallucination" special value for Breton. At the same time the qualifying adjective "voluntary" makes it plain that the form of hallucination which commands his admiration is not the uncontrolled liberty of the mind unhinged, refusing to come to terms with the real. He advocates, rather, deliberate surrender on the part of the poet to hallucinatory experience made possible by willing abandon of the control exercised by reason over habitual thought. In the exciting rearrangement of the elements which habit would persuade us to view in a conventional order the poet must safeguard himself against the danger of a vain pursuit of private obsession. For he must be an explorer bold enough to advance into the interior of thought, beyond the peripheral regions over which reason reigns; and he must report his findings through poetic statement. His poem signposts his journey, without giving any guarantee that those who care to follow behind will find their experience enriched by what he can show them.

We must not forget in this connection that *L'Immaculée Conception* invites us to take inspiration from the spaces between the lines, and that Eluard has written that poems always have big white margins, "margins of silence"—a silence which, clearly, we ourselves must break. And so Breton's reference to the function of language as "not to communicate" would be misinterpreted, if viewed as authority for incomprehensibility. Breton shuns commonplace communication, in which meaningless banalities are exchanged by persons indifferent to the press-

[44]

ing need to transform the world. Such a form of communication must be replaced with another, aimed at promoting a perception of reality that owes more to inner vision than to external contingency.

Perhaps what impresses most about André Breton's work is its unity, ensured by more than forty years of fidelity to surrealism. Breton spoke for surrealism in such resounding tones that even today those who find it all too easy to disregard the contribution to surrealist theory of Aragon, Eluard, Mabille, and Péret consider Breton to be surrealism's only spokesman. They tend to forget that he did not once speak as a mere theorist. Any discoveries he shares with us he first made for himself, and what he has to tell us he first had to learn for himself. His essays are statements of poetic aspiration to which his verses lend full meaning. Both essay and poem serve to express a view of existence, projecting a special faith and hope. Whatever text of Breton's we open, we find the same beliefs, the same determination to surmount obstacles which to many of us seem insurmountable. Casting off the pessimistic conclusions to which immediate circumstance would reduce us, Breton's work offers the promise, at least, of a serene vision of striking optimism, sufficient in itself to guarantee Breton a special place among twentieth-century French writers. In 1948 he brought his selected *Poèmes* to a close with "Sur la route de San Romano." Fittingly, this poem ends with three lines which sum up a whole lifetime of poetic effort, set it in perspective, and ensure it our respect:

> The poetic embrace like the embrace of the flesh
> While it lasts
> Protects against any glimpse of the misery of the world.

SELECTED BIBLIOGRAPHY

PRINCIPAL WORKS OF ANDRÉ BRETON

Mont de Piété. Paris, Au Sans Pareil, 1919.

Clair de Terre. Paris, Collection Littérature, 1923.

Les Pas perdus. Paris, Editions de la N.R.F., 1924.

Manifeste du Surréalisme, Poisson soluble. Paris, Aux Editions du Sagittaire, chez Simon Kra, 1924.

Introduction au Discours sur le Peu de Réalité. Paris, Gallimard, 1927.

Nadja. Paris, Edition de la N.R.F., 1928; rev. ed., Paris, Gallimard, 1963. (Nadja. Tr. Richard Howard. New York, Grove Press, 1960.)

Le Surréalisme et la Peinture. Paris, Editions de la N.R.F., 1928; enl. ed., New York, Brentano's, 1945; enl. ed., Paris, Gallimard, 1965.

Second Manifeste du Surréalisme. Paris, Kra, 1930.

L'Union libre. Paris, Editions surréalistes, 1931.

Le Revolver à Cheveux blancs. Paris, Editions des Cahiers libres, 1932.

Les Vases communicants. Paris, Editions des Cahiers libres, 1932.

L'Air de l'Eau. Paris, Editions d'Art, 1934.

Point du Jour. Paris, Gallimard, 1934.

Qu'est-ce que le Surréalisme? Brussels, Henriquez, 1934. (What Is Surrealism? Tr. David Gascoyne. London, Faber, 1936.)

Position politique du Surréalisme. Paris, Editions du Sagittaire, 1935.

L'Amour fou. Paris, Gallimard, 1937.

Anthologie de l'Humour noir. Paris, Editions du Sagittaire, 1940; enl. ed., 1950.

Arcane 17. New York, Brentano's, 1944; reprinted Paris, Le Sagittaire, 1947.

Situation du Surréalisme entre les deux Guerres. Paris, Editions de la revue Fontaine, 1945.

Les Manifestes du Surréalisme suivi de Prolégomènes à un Troisième Manifeste du Surréalisme ou Non. Paris, Le Sagittaire, 1946.

Ode à Charles Fourier. Paris, Editions de la revue Fontaine, 1947.

La Lampe dans l'Horloge. Paris, Editions Robert Marin, 1948.

Poèmes. Paris, Gallimard, 1948.

Entretiens 1913–1952. Paris, N.R.F., 1952.

La Clé des Champs. Paris, Editions du Sagittaire, 1953.

Adieu ne Plaise. Alès, P.A.B., 1954.

Les Manifestes du Surréalisme suivi de Prolégomènes à un Troi-

sième Manifeste du Surréalisme ou Non, du Surréalisme en ses
Œuvres vives et d'Ephémérides surréalistes. Paris, Le Sagittaire,
1955.

Le La. Alès, P.A.B., 1961.

Premier Manifeste, Second Manifeste, Prolégomènes à un Troisième
Manifeste du Surréalisme ou Non, Position politique du Sur-
réalisme [extracts], Poisson soluble, Lettre aux Voyantes, Du
Surréalisme en ses Œuvres vives. Paris, Pauvert, 1962.

Manifestes du Surréalisme. Paris, Gallimard, 1963.

PRINCIPAL WORKS IN COLLABORATION

Les Champs magnétiques (with Philippe Soupault). Paris, Au Sans
Pareil, 1920.

Ralentir Travaux (with René Char and Paul Eluard). Paris, Editions surréalistes, 1930.

L'Immaculée Conception (with Paul Eluard). Paris, Editions surréalistes (chez José Corti), 1930; reprinted Paris, Seghers, 1961.

Notes sur la Poésie (with Paul Eluard). Paris, G.L.M., 1936.

Pour un Art révolutionnaire indépendant (with Leon Trotsky,
though Diego Rivera's name appears on the cover). Mexico, July
25, 1938.

First Papers of Surrealism (with Marcel Duchamp). New York,
Coordinating Council of French Relief, 1942.

Martinique Charmeuse de Serpents (with André Masson). Paris, Le
Sagittaire, 1948.

L'Art magique (with Gérard Legrand). Paris, Formes et Couleurs,
1957.

CRITICAL WORKS AND COMMENTARY

NOTE: *Books only are listed.*

Ode à Charles Fourier, commentée par Jean Gaulmier. Paris,
Klincksieck, 1961.

Bédouin, Jean-Louis. André Breton. Paris, Pierre Seghers, Collection "Poètes d'Aujourd'hui," 1950.

Carrouges, Michel. André Breton et les Données fondamentales du
Surréalisme. Paris, Gallimard, 1950.

Caws, Mary Ann. Surrealism and the Literary Imagination: A Study
of Breton and Bachelard. The Hague, Mouton, 1966.

Crastre, Victor. André Breton. Paris, Arcanes, 1952.

Eideldinger, Marc, ed. André Breton: Essais et Témoignages.
Neuchâtel, à la Baconnière, 1950.

Gracq, Julien. André Breton: Quelques Aspects de l'Ecrivain. Paris, 1948.
Mauriac, Claude. André Breton. Paris, Editions de Flore, 1949.